FROM BELLSHILL TO CHARLEROI

From the Journal of Andrew Addie, 1923

Transcribed and formatted by
Robert & Nicole Du Shane

HOPKIN'S HOUSE
PUBLISHING

ISBN: 978-1-52271-380-7

Library of Congress CIP data applied for.

First Edition: December 2015

This Journal was written by Andrew Addie during his voyage to America with his wife and young son in 1923.

The journal was transcribed exactly as written and no corrections to spelling, capitalization, or grammar were made.

There is a small glossary in the back of the book to define some words that may be unfamiliar,

From Glasgow, Scotland to Ellis Island, New York

September 26, 1923

After having parted with loved ones, we entered the enclosure for 3rd Class passengers, where we received a card which we are to keep a hold of during the voyage. This is known as the "landing card."

Later on, women and children are admitted to mother enclosure for Medical Inspections before going aboard. While the men are waiting to go in, a gentleman is busy writing cards of introduction to the Y.M.C.A. in New York for any one who wants them, so I got one thinking it might come in handy. Later on our time arrives for Medical Inspection. In we go, "Hats and coats off, please, uncover arm and show vaccination." When ready we pass in one by one to a place screened off, in which a Doctor is waiting. He looks at your arm and stamps your card, then on you go again to another Doctor who has a look at your hands, also your eyes. Sometimes he has a look at the head, it all depends who is passing. I had no trouble whatever. We get our clothes on again, and pass out to board the ship.

Again our card is stamped. When we get aboard the stewards are waiting to take you to your cabin, one number being on this card you get. Nan and James getting on the boat first they find the cabin first, the steward carrying James down the stairs. When I get down the steward is waiting;

"What's your number, sir?" I hand him the card. "Follow me."
I follow him to the cabin we are to occupy during the voyage.

"Well Mack, I'll tell you what you should do."
"What?"
"You had better sleep on top here, and let the missus and son sleep here," pointing to Beds 2&4.
"Right oh! Steward."
"I'll be your steward during the voyage."
"Right Sir. I'll see you later on"
"It's alright Mack."

After getting my coat off, I get upstairs to have a farewell wave to friends. After a while they all leave, so we walk about the deck having a look around. The first place I find out is the Dining Saloon, then then Lavatories, in which are wash-hand basins, W.C.'s Spray baths, towels, soap, etc., Hot & Cold water in every place.

At 3 o'clock bell rings for tea, and of course we get off our mark and are there about first, getting seated next to the pantry. For tea we have stew and potatoes, rice and prunes. Plenty of everything.

Pass the remainder of the time on deck making many friends. One chap, Tom Ogilvie, a fine fellow married sixteen months ago and have been one on of the Anchor Liners for a while, give me a tip or two. One especially. He told me to give no tips at all at the beginning, they don't trouble you much after, but if you don't, they do all in their power for you. Tom and I talk for a while. Talk about the Craft, Work, where we have been, married life and many other things.

All at once two women cry "Come here you men quick, one of the attendants have been away getting drunk." When he returns he finds the gangway is drawn, and first makes a spring at the railings. He manages to get a hold and is hanging there, when Tom and I give him a lift up. He signs to the others standing by to say nothing.

Eight o'clock comes and the bell rings once again for supper. Coffee, biscuits and cheese. Biscuits very hard, cheese splendid, coffee very nice. This over, we get up on the deck again waiting on the boat moving off, crowds still hang around to have a final look at this great ship as it leaves.

At 10 P.M. sharp operations commence. The tender gets out of the way ready to drop in behind when the tug gets far enough down to let her do so. Off we go slowly. Before this at 9:30 all women are ordered below, no women allowed on deck, men allowed to remain. We are busy watching all movements. Crowds with torches along both banks cheer us as we pass.

When we get to Renfrew 10.40 p.m. the Banks are packed with people cheering and shouting many things; everybody in good spirits. John Murphy is with us now; that is the fellow we were introduced to by Sanny Fuller. I make a suggestions we get to bed.

"Very good," says Tom.

"Well," says Murphy, "We'll see him home." So we went along

the corridor to the other side of the boat with Tom, then came back and got into bed.

***

Well the first night I didn't sleep well, the throb of the engines kept me from sleeping. I dose off, waken up to look my watch, 3 a.m. so tuck in again; don't remember until rattle at the door:

> *"Time you were up 6 o'clock, breakfast at 7."*
> *"Right on," I said.*
> *"Alright, Mack," replied the Steward.*

We get up and get washed, waiting for the Bell to go. Here we are about first again down at the Saloon, Tables ready waiting, Stewards and Attendants all over. We have a chair each, chair are like the Barbers', can turn right round about (much to James' liking).

Breakfast we have Hamm and Egg with mashed potato, Rolls, Bread, Butter, Jam, etc., a great luck in.

On Deck once more watching the Irish Free State as we pass up the Loon to Moville, where we stop to take on passengers. We are lying out in the water of course, and the Boat "Lady Clare" comes along side with passengers and luggage. We are at the side of the boat watching all coming on, amused at the Irish brogue of the Captain of "Lady Clare;" a cranky old man, ever ready for "Lady Clare" to draw away.

3 or 4 of us draw one of the ropes of the standards and let go. Now they are taking the depth of water before we turn to go down the Loon again

4

and make for the West.

Ireland out of sight we have boat drill, as usual I am away from my quarters. A Sailor comes to me and whispers in my ear "Down and get your Life Belt on." I have to toddle away to the other end of the boat where everybody has a Life Belt on but our James, and he won't have one on at no cost; the Nurse said, "Never mind the wee one just now." When all ready up stairs to the Boat Deck where we all muster; all there, we are told this is where we have to come when the Bugle sounds.

Dinner time arrives, Broth, Potatoes, Roast Pork, Rice, Prunes, plenty of everything, finished up with an apple.

At 2p.m. we have to go to the Ladies' Room with the Ocean Ticket and Passport; we, Murphy and I have been along a few times but the place is full up, we come back and wait for a while until we thinking everybody has gone.

Murphy won't stay. People sick all over. Boat pitching, we are getting a great laugh at the Sea Sicks, especially one man who is lying on a form all out, roaring like a Calf. Every now and then he tries to get some of his dinner up, as he is doing so, another Irishman, also sick, keeps shouting at him "Stick it, stick it." I nearly fall laughing.

I am in the room waiting to get the table with my Passport, still six in front of me. Alas I must go, a Bee Line for the Lavatory, get the door open in time when I let go with vengeance. Dinner and all the rest has reappeared, I could not keep it down at all.

Mr. Harvey says, "There is nothing like a sea voyage to bring out a man what's in him."

The place was too stuffy, I got back to the Room and sat down.

"Alas Walker you're on the move to I see it coming." This is a fellow I met at Glasgow, was in the Navy for 4 years, a Painter to Trade.

I saw him later on and asked him how he felt when he got out of the room. "Oh," says he, "I had to make straight for the W. C. before my turn came, I got the door opened but I forgot everything then, when I came to I was on my knees and all my dinner lying before me again, what went down last came up first." I laughed at him telling his story.

I came back to see how Nan and James were keeping, Nan was sick before this and James had to let go once, and then he was all right. When I got along to them Nan and another chap were counseling one another about sea sickness. Says I "I am just after letting go."
Nan says, "Are you sick too?"

I said, "I am not so bad now," but I had to toe the line 3 times after that.

Tea time came, no attraction for us, very few for tea, everybody sick, even the crew, some of them; our stewardess was sick too.
The nurse came round the cabins with tea and buns. James is in the pink, never sick at all (only vomited once). He has got tea from the nurse, but he is off again hunting for her with his tinnie, "More tea," he says. We get into bed.

Murphy he is neither up nor down. He is running carrying drinks to the sick. He does so until 2 a.m. Takes off his boots and runs about in his bare feet. I haven't seen Tom for a day. I am afraid he is over the clog too.

***

Friday morning. Bell goes for breakfast, but neither Nan or I are fit to face the music. James he is wanting to get his breakfast. Later on I scramble out of bed, get on my clothes, take James down to the Saloon.

> *I get one of the attendants to the door and asks him if he would give the wee chap a piece as he has had no breakfast.*
> *'Right forward to the pantry and you'll get anything you want."*
> *I went to the pantry and made known my errand.*
> *"Well, what do you want?"*
> *"A piece of bread please,"*
> *I got two slice of bread with butter and jam, so James laid round him.*

Nan, James and I got to the back of the boat and got seated in the air. Boat still pitching, water choppy, lovely day.

I have a talk with a fellow who comes from Uddingston, used to work in Clydesdale, was in U.S.A. before, and was a victim of the day before too. I tell you it's great hearing all the stories.

Dinner times comes. We are going to try it, so off we go, but only to be told we must come back for the second sitting, as tickets were issued in the morning for seats at the table. We waited to the second sitting, went down, got our tickets for the seats at the table. Our numbers are strange to say 111, 112, 113.

Nearly all young men beside us, and they don't forget James. They always say "Here Jack" (chipping down a bun or something else) "put that in your pocket for the wee chap." They wanted me to bring a jug of milk with me. The chap from Uddingston nits next to me at the table. Bags of grub.

At the root of the menu card is printed "If you don't get enough food, please make it known to the Chief Steward," but there is no room to grumble about the food nor the way it is cooked. I got the surprise of my life. Plants on the table and everything you could mention nearly.

I got on not so bad at dinner, lentil soup. I had two helpings, it was splendid. That was all I had, determined to take a little, but to keep a hold of it, which I did. James wanted potatoes, so I waited with him. Nan went upstairs when got her soup for fear she would have to part with it again.

We passed the remainder of the afternoon lying on deck, which was nice and dry, the sun shining lovely. Still we are riding over the Atlantic Rollers, boat still heaving, but we don't mind that now.
"What's that?" A rush for the side of the boat. 3 Dole Fish appear jumping out of the water, and diving in again. They were almost within 10 yards of the boat, but didn't come up far, they soon let off. Later we say sea-swallows. They sleep in the seas I suppose, but follow the passing ships for a bit and then give up.

Tea time comes at which we can have Fish, Cold Meat, pickles, tea, bread, buns, pudding and apricots. I had fish, then apricots and milk.

We then got sprawled on out deck again. Walker is beside me. Another chap comes to him and asks him if he will play for a few dances. Walkers can play a violin to some tune, so he consented. I got down and listened to the music while the others skipped about the deck. Then we had a change in the programme, a few songs, nearly all scotch. Then there were another change, all the company singing choruses. At 7.30 as the sing song was going on, one girls says "Look, what's yonder?" It was the lights of a passing tramp steamer, the first we had seen since we left Ireland.

For three hours to-day the "California" did 78 miles. We got a wireless that the "Cameronia" was 200 miles in front in a storm. 'Good Luck' to it. It must have taken it with it, as we have got none of it so far.

At 8 o'clock, downstairs to bed, never went to supper. All in our beds when the wee steward comes along, "How are all here?"

"Not bad Steward."

"You had better take some milk for the Baby."

I handed him James' tinnie. He filled it up and left it on the seat saying, "good night. I'll see you in the morning."

Oh! Yes, I nearly forgot to say that I went down to the bar looking for Soda Water, but found none. They only had ginger, so I got two bottles, which cost 8d each, small bottles. A shave costs 9d, haircut 1/9d, very reasonable!!! I wonder if they know it's Scotland we come from.

***

Saturday. We feel much better. Nan is up first then James. He comes up into the bunk beside me while his mother is away getting washed. Time 6.30. After that James goes to get washed. I get up and get shaved, and then all three have a walk along the boat waiting on the bell going.

Ting-a-ling, there is goes. Oh! my, mince and potatoes for breakfast, rolls, etc. My, I gave it a scrutoning. I tell you. More at the tables this morning, all the folks are getting over their sickness. The deck was crowded this morning, many up there for the first time since we left Glasgow. One chap has never been to the Saloon since he left Glasgow until to-day.

Breakfast past, we had a walk right up to the front of the boat, couldn't go any further. I have been up in both 1st and 2nd Class. No one spoke a word. It's much nicer done up right enough; they get black grapes, etc., and we don't, still we can't grumble. Yet, any one that can afford it should come 2nd Class. However, all the talk about 3rd Class passengers being examined every day is only a lot of stuff, no such thing.

The steward is round washing the floor and polishing the brasses, etc., making the beds. Nan squared off the beds one morning but when we came in after being out, they were all altered. They have their own way of making them up, and they must be made up that way, because they never know when the Captain or Doctor is coming round to inspect the cabins to see they are kept clean and proper. That is to make the stewards attend to their work. Any one not able to be out of bed, the Nurse attends them, carries all to them, what ever they require. I tell you, you would be surprised if you could only see everything in working order here.

About 10 p.m. this morning, all who were not sick were to go upstairs. The Captain, Doctor, Purser and other 3 Officers were round all the Cabins inspecting them, also W.C. and Wash Basins, etc. I may say there is a basin in every cabin, but only used when sick, or if you wish you can carry in the water and wash, but when you are able, they like you to go upstairs. If not they turn on the water for you. The water pipels led into the basin, and all closes up neatly with mirror at top, 18" long x one foot broad. Pegs at either side of mirror and also door, plenty of room and accommodation. No great crowds waiting at wash basins to get washed, as reported in the Old Country. Go when you like you can get in, despite the fact the "California" is carrying 260 passengers in 1st Class, 461 in 2nd Class, 1,000 in 3rd Class and 345 of a crew, in all 2066. A nice gathering could hold many more. Not so many passengers this time, and the crew is also smaller.

Another thing, one can go into the cook house at all times, and they will give you whatever you want, tea, steak, milk, anything, they charge nothing, but leave it to yourself.

Many of the young men and women are playing at jumping ropes, also Blind Man's Bluff. While playing at the latter they say that any one who goes overboard is out!!! Ha! Ha!

There are a crowd of comics on the boat. Master-at-Arms (or police) gave them ropes and at night if it is getting rather dark, and him nearby, he switches on the deck light. I believe you will be thinking it is hardly true, but it is a fact. They will do anything for you.

It is a long day I admit, 6 a.m. until 10 p.m. Of course you can go to bed when you like.

The stewards start at 5 a.m. and stop at 11 p.m. A long day for them. I asked the steward when he was in to-day how he stuck it. "Oh," he said, "if it was not for the money that is in it, I wouldn't be here." He has been fourteen years at sea. Young fellow he is, I don't think he will be much older than myself.

As he was leaving, the two nurses come along and said, "Well, steward how are you to-day?"

> *"Rotten Nurse."*
> *"What's the trouble?"*
> *"Fed up polishing brasses with emery cloth."*
> *"But see what a good man you will make steward."*
> *"I'll be nobody's man," he replied.*

"Why?"

"I've no girl."

"Well, can we do anything for you," asked the nurse. "We will do our utmost."

"Well," he said. "You can get me a girl with grey eyes, and a curly nose."

"Anything else?"

"About your own height, speak a little thicker than you."

"One fat or lean?"

"Yes, one that will keep me warm at night," he said.

"Alright we will be on the lookout."

They have some fun together.

Dinner. We have roast mutton, potatoes, (soup first) pudding, and slices of water melon, only from two to four inches thick. It is like the ordinary melon only is is red in the inside, green skin, much juicier and "wereh" tasted, fine for doing away with thirst.

After we get that over, another walk along the corridor, which is like walking from the top of the row to the foot of it. While away the time watching the jumping ropes, etc., then I come down and write for a while.

There's the bell for the first sitting. James is ready for it, but we can't go before our turn, so we get up on deck and have a walk until our time comes. It's a lovely night.

Could you guess what is on the menu for tea? "Steak Pie." Yam! Yam! We saw them to-day in the cook house in basins, about 3 feet in lengths, one of these and a board of bread, a cistern of tea, would give a fellow a decent meal.

Tea time. We did enjoy it. Steak pie and potatoes, bread, buns, tea, and pudding. "Teeth watering, eh?" It's great reading this.
One chap at the table said, 'Well, if I can't knock out Jack Dempsey after this when I get over, well it's not my fault."

James wants a dose, I think so does his mother, for they are both sound asleep now. I have the cabin trunk for a seat, and the cabin seat for a table or desk.

The steward at the door again.
> *'Excuse me Sir" he says, "how many in here?"*
> *"Three," I replied.*
> *"Your wife?"*
> *"Yes."*
> *"Youself?"*
> *"Yes"*
> *"And the boy?"*
> *I said, "yes."*
> *"How old is he?"*
> *"Four years"*
> *"I will put him down as a child, not as a baby, and you will get through quicker."*

All under six years are babies according to their way of looking at things. He is off now.

Hark! Music. "Sleep on beloved and take thy rest." I am up the stair to the music. "First set," I hear them say. Sweet dreams Nan and James, I'm off.

When I get up the dancing is going ahead. Dulcimer and violin in one place, a violin in another, pipes in another, plenty of music, in fact third class is the liveliest of the boat. Second class passengers come down here too to enjoy the fun. There is a concert down here at 2.30 p.m. to-day and many of the knuts from above came down to it.

While the run was at it's pitch, I noticed something away behind the boat. In the darkness I couldn't understand what it was, but I kept a keen eye on it. It appeared like a ray of light on the water at first, then it rose gradually till it appeared like a flame or fire. Later on it came into full view - - it was the MOON. What a lovely sight. You would think it just rose out of the water, when it was just about a foot above the water, as it looked to us. It sent a glimmer along the water. I never could enjoy looking at a picture "Moonlight at Sea," as they usually call them, until I saw it for myself. It was a great sight.

After talking to another chap for a while, I bid him good-night and make for the cabin. I get into bed and enjoyed my night's sleep.

***

Sunday. Getting up I find the ship is not pitching so much, or maybe we have just got our "sealegs." We can walk about as good as the sailors now.

Breakfast time arrives. Porridge, we have that first thing every morning, Bacon and Eggs, please note "eggs." I had to wait for a while on mining coming, so the steward made up with an extra egg for me. American Dry Hash, rolls, bread, butter, Jam, etc.

James was waiting at the top of the stairs for the bell to go.

Now he is waiting on his dinner because he knows there is ice cream after dinner to-day. We get chicken soup, Fowl and potatoes, vegetables, pudding and ice cream bis-nap, not a bad tack in, eh?

While I am writing this we are in the General Room, which is furnished with table and chairs, where one can write, read or play any of the table games. It is nicely done off. Wood work all neatly paneled, glass door, pictures on the walls.

Another tramp steamer has passed while we were down for dinner. The water is rough again, and it is very hazy around.

I was asking Nan what the folks in the Old Country would be doing. I looked my watch and it was 3.25, but to this we must add 2 hours 40 minutes to get the correct time on the land we left behind. Since we left Ireland our watches have been put back 25 minutes each day, so that when we arrive at New York, we will be right with their time.

After leaving Ireland, we passed through a bit called the "Devil's Hole," where four different waters meet. I forgot to mention this earlier in my letter.

I had a talk with a fellow to-day who comes from Motherwell, and he pointed out two chaps who came from Holytown. There are an awful lot of young men on this Boat, many of them not long married.
I thought there would have been a service to-day but I don't hear anything about one, unless there is one up in second class quarters.
It is five o'clock now, Nan is lying on top of clothes in the Bottom Bunk. We are just after eating two rare big juicy oranges, my word they were grand! Nan is asking me to go to the pantry and get more. James is out there playing at the root of the stairs with other wee ones.

Later on we spent a while on deck. James went off to sleep while we were sitting on one of the Standards at the back of the Boat. The sea is very heavy and we are getting a good heave.

Tea time comes and we are on the dot. Fish or Cold Meat, Rice and Prunes.

We spend the remainder of the night on deck. The sea is still very heavy, indeed it looks like being a rough night. James is ready for bed, so Nan takes him away and gives him a salt water bath, and tucks him in.
I met Walker again and we have a great talk, he is a great "Wag" right enough, a right comic. I nearly kicked laughing at him. He can fairly imitate the Irishman, and also the Auld Sooton Man; when he gets going he would keep you in fits.

While we are talking another big fellow comes forward and joins us, I don't know his name as yet, but a very fine fellow. His wife has never been right since she boarded the Ship. We had a great time together.

The waves are fairly lashing up now. I mentioned it to one of the Stewards about the heavy sea, "Oh!" says he. "We are off the Banks of NewFoundland, that's the cause." We'll get better weather every day now. He says about other three days will finish up, and I would not mind I can tell you, for this is a lazy life, and I think there are many more forby me would like to be landed. Not that it is too rough, but nothing to do and it is such a long day.

Well we bid each other Adieu, and make for our bunks. I have only been for coffee once , for I feel I don't need it. Plenty without it, so I don't want to over do it.

Nobody can say they are starved on this boat. Nurse and Doctor are at your disposal if you require them, Free Medicine, Bandages, etc., if you are in need of them.

***

I have a good sleep and at 5 a.m. awaken; what's the trouble now, the engines are not going, but I am so much alarmed at this I turn on my way other side and go off to sleep, knowing if it is anything serious we will get to know in due time. About forty minutes the engines are started again.

Here comes that Steward again, 'Time you were up," so we have to jump once more for another day's prowling about. I get my razor strapped go upstairs and shave, wash and get dressed.

Make for Deck, meet Walker. He tells me the Steering Gear had got stuck this morning that was the cause of the engines being stopped. He came up the stair to see what had happened, so the Master-at-Arms told him what the trouble was. It hadn't been getting properly oiled and it had jammed somehow. Whoever is to blame will likely get into trouble as we lost two hours.

Breakfast bell goes, I'm off at the double and arrive first at the table. Nan and James come when I have my porridge finished. Then sausages and Bacon and Mashed Potato.

At ten o'clock we have Medical Inspection which takes place in the Dining saloon. Women and children first then the "mere" men later on. An Official comes along the corridor. "Follow me lads." Down we get, place is packed. Doctor and Attendants come in and a rush is made to get examine first.

Tommy Wilson, from Motherwell, and I sit and wait until all the est are down, then comes our turn. We pass two Officials who take the number of our Medical card, then another one looks both of our hands, then the Chief Doctor looks at the back of the neck. All over and upstairs. Simply nothing.

The women get the sides of their heads looked, that is all, I think.

I am waiting on the Dinner bell sounding so I will stop meantime and put this book of tales out of the way for the present. So long!

Had a very nice dinner to-day. Roast Beef, Lamb, Potatoes and Cabbage, Sago and Water Melon.

I was very hungry to-day, and I fairly enjoyed it.

Then we had a seat at the rear of the boat. Nan took James downstairs to see if he would take a sleep. John Murphy and I have a walk up to the very nose of the boat, watching the man in the Crow's Nest for a while, and then the Captain on the Bridge. It is really a wonderful boat the "California." If you know any one coming out to America, or in fact anyone taking a sea voyage, tell them never to forget the Health salts, or Acid or Lemon Drops. The water is not good on the boat.

On Friday last, I went up to the Barber on the second deck, and got a bottle of Saline 2/-, and a bottle of Lemon Drops 1/8d. Still we are glad to get them. The only thing I don't care much for is the water.

Any old clothes do for the boat. I have never had a collar on unless Sunday. Many of the chaps have on the oldest clothes they could get their hands on, some of them patched. Of course, upstairs, they are always a little swanky. Comfort and ease first, eh?

The sky is a bit clearer now, and one could see a ship a good bit away. There was another ship passed while we were in the dining saloon. I notice

also many more sea gulls are flying about, so we must be coming nearer land.

***

Well, this is Wednesday now. I did not manage to get any writing done yesterday. On Monday at four p.m. a storm arose, and I can tell you we didn't half get it. The sea was mountains high, much higher than the ship, big and all as it is.

Tuesday night at 10 p.m. the storm was very bad, a wave swept the top deck, broke of a ventilator and smashed in one of the port holes. It staggered the ship to some tune. We were all in bed, and whenever we felt the thud, we thought all was up. I thought it was another Titanic disaster. No lifeboat could live in such a sea, when this one 17,000 tons was bobbing about like a cork. It just looked like us running against a rock.

Our stewardess was tossed out of bed, and she got such a fright, this she put her pinkie in her mouth and bit it through. She let me see it the next morning.

There are some laughs now it is passed. Two Irishmen in their pyjamas suits, boots in their pockets, landing card in one hand, suitcase in the other, and made for the lifeboat. Had it really been anything serious they would not have required their landing cards. They would have landed alright without them.

Many of the women got up in night attire and rushed for the corridor. I could hear quite clearly one of the officials saying, "Tell the women to get back to bed, it is alright."

We never rose at all, knowing it was useless, as nothing could have saved us. Everybody got a fright I can tell you. Fancy the waves being higher than the funnel of this boat! This lasted all night Monday night, all day Tuesday, and was very bad when we went to bed on Tuesday night. I don't know when it calmed down, but on Wednesday morning when we awoke, what a change! No heaving, no wild winds, and when we got up on deck, what a beautiful morning, sun shining bright, sea as calm as can be.

It is very warm to-day, I believe the best day I have seen for the last two years. You would fairly enjoy this sail to-day, blue sky above, blue sea below, and a blazing sun. It is lovely indeed.

I saw smoke coming from another ship away on our right, but up till now it has not appeared in sight.

James awakened this morning at 4 o'clock and the first question was "Who is Charlie Chaplin?" He is sticking it alright and enjoying himself. All thought he would have got a fright when he saw the waves so high, but he didn't trouble.

We get our money changed to-day at 4 P.M.

Some of the women who are troubled with dandruff in the hair, are getting hair drill daily so that they will pass at Ellis Island.

We had mince and mashed potatoes at breakfast to-day. Last night at tea we had herring, fine big ones too, and we have ice cream after dinner and an apple. We are just waiting for the dinner bell going again, and we'll enjoy it better to-day.

There are some or two who have never been out of bed since they left Glasgow. One woman they tried up on deck this morning, but she fainted clean away, and they worked with her for 15 minutes trying to get her round, but had to carry her down stairs at the latter end. I don't know how they got on with her, but she was an awful sight. Later report about this woman – she managed up on deck again and keeping a little better.

We had a nice dinner to-day, potato soup, potatoes and roast beef and beans, and pudding.

We then had a seat on deck, it was really lovely to-day. I expected having a bath, but the day was too good, I didn't want to lose any of it.

The Nan and I had a walk up to the Barber's and later on, we went along the purser and got the remainder of our money changed.
Then had a talk with Walker and Tom Ogilvie, and later on with George McKenzie a chap from Uddingston.

Then the tea bell went and we had steak and onions and lettuce and to finish up with we have rice and rhubarb.

The just got back on to deck when we saw a boat making for the Homeland. It looked like a large cargo boat.

After that the dancing started once again. All the Irish people stick together on this boat, so they had a dance of their own. While this was going on, I et in with an Orangemen from Motherwell, he used to carry the stick in front of the County Corner Band, a well made fellow indeed.

I will ring off again and go and get some water for cocoa. "Could you take a bun, eh?"

We must be drawing near America now, as I notice the darkness falls all at once.

✵✵✵

This is now Thursday and it is a lovely day. I was up on the front deck before breakfast and it was lovely, no breeze at all, would hardly know the ship was going at all. Then I heard seven bells going, that was half past seven, so I thought I better make down to the dining room, as the second bell would soon be going.

We had ham and egg, dry hash.

After getting this lot out of sight we went up to the front deck again. There was more of a breeze this time.

Then the man in the Crow's Nest sounded the bell, which means something in sight. Whenever he sees anything he sounds the bell, so we had a look round and saw something way ahead of us, but couldn't make out what it was. As we came nearer we found it was a sailing ship. Just after that we saw the "Nantucket Light ship," and while after we saw another smaller ship pass, No. 8 was on the side of it.

Watching these ships I missed a "fly" cup of tea. Nan and one or two other women has a tea party of their own,, and then they say they were all over the ship looking for me. Well, I'll guarantee I wasn't out of it any way! I feel in the pink to-day and could eat a horse I am so hungry.

James has just shouted in "There's the first bell Father." I wish it was the second. I bet there won't be too many "tatties" left to-day and many other things. You folks will be taking a notion of a trip.

Across here when you hear of all the good things.

I sat until 10.15 p.m. on deck last night talking to the two table stewards. Of course, 'birds of a Feather flock together." Square men as usual!

All the women were down stairs at 9 p.m. Morality is the reason. One young woman from 2nd class ventured down her after the hour with her young chap, but once the Master-at-Arms got his eyes on her, she soon retracted her footsteps, and all the stewards and many of the male passengers were sitting on deck. The Master-at-Arms kept her at her heels all the time until she got upstairs.

If any thing takes place out of the way on the ship, it's peoples own fault. Once before the Captain made a young couple get married before they left the ship because of their carry on. The young woman did not want to do so but she had to do it or be deported. People may do as they like thinking no one is watching, but at the end of the voyage, their whole behavior could be given. These fellows don't walk about with their eyes shut.

Well, I will now jump a bit and say more about the voyage. Thursday night we came to the Hudson River. We saw many ships lying around and it was a lovely sight. I can tell you.

Then we passed "Fire Island" on our right (or starboard side) on your left (or Port side) Jersey, and the places being all lit up it was a beautiful sight.

Then on our left again Coney Island and Long island. This would be about 7.30 p.m. We stood on the fore deck all evening. It was very exciting.

Then we took on the Pilot and he took the ship up the River to Quarentine, where we cast anchor at 10.30 p.m. and remained there all night.

✳✳✳

In the morning we were up and ready for the Doctor at 6.30 a.m. (Friday). The ship could not move up to New York until the inspection took place. The Doctor, an American of course, just examined one or two men, and then said that would do. The women were put through it too.

When the Doctor left the ship, we went up to where the ship had to be berthed, so we are now waiting to be taken to Ellis Island. We won't get off until to-morrow.

The "Mauretania" came along side of us at Quarantine this morning but we got up before her. It is not such a big boat as I thought it was.

It was a nice sight coming up the River this morning in the sunshine and every kind of boat floating about here and Stars and Stripes in galore.
I think I will now close and get this posted. We are in the pink.

From New York to Charleroi, via Pittsburg, Pennsylvania

While waiting at New York until our turn came to go to the Ellis Island, we spent thetime watching the men unloading the cargo. At the back end of the boat there was a barge unloading apples. Whenever the men came across a barrel that was damaged they didn't forget to land a few apples on to the deck of the "California," to the delight of us all. In fact had it been a barrel at a time instead of an apple, it would not have worried us in the least.

On Saturday morning at 5.30 a.m. we had breakfast for the last time on the "California." Afterwards we had to get ready for leaving the ship.

The all ready, bags in hand, we got on to the second deck ready to go ashore. One by one we crossed the gangway, all the while the ship's Master-at-Arms and one or two other officials bidding us goodbye.

At the Customs sheds we were arranged in rows with our bags lying open in front of us. The officers came along examined him, put the mark on and passed on. I was lucky enough to get mine passed without being ransacked.

Then we had to claim our large boxes and trunks, have them examined and marked also. Again no trouble. It was a colored officer that looked at ours. He asked me what was in the big box. I said, "Household utensils."

"That's alright," marked it, looked the name and said "What's wrong your name is not Mac?" For nearly every one that comes here is a Mac."

We got our boxes roped up and taken over to get checked. Checks are put every box you have, and you get a check for each one also when you go to claim them at your journey's end. You must produce the checks before you get them.

Then we were taken to Ellis Island. We had to wait a good while ere we got landing, then our turn came and it was only 10 minutes after we got into the large hall that attendants came and gave us sandwiches and coffee. It was splendid I can tell you and we all enjoyed it. The children got milk and biscuits.

Then we went out in single file and passed the doctors. One would look your eyes, hand and pass you, unless you were minus a finger, then a chalk mark was put on your coat, and when you went further along, you had to go into a room for further examination.

Then upstairs into another great big hall, and I can tell you it was spotless, with two large American Flags hanging from the centre, so that it is impossible for anyone to pass through Ellis Island without passing under the Stars and Stripes.

There were clerks, etc., here to whom you had to show your passport and answer one or two questions. Then pass on to the Booking Hall, the worst part of the Island in my opinion. Bags are left in the centre of the hall, and you go over to one counter where train slip is examined and marked O.K. Then it is taken to another counter, where you get a ticket for it.

After you have your ticket, there are one or two officials who would like to hustle you out of the hall. One came along to me and said, "Come on now, if you have got your ticket, get out of this."

I turned and said, "Take your time, you won't hustle me."

When he saw how I took it, he said, "Oh! It's alright Mac," and he turned and went away.

I got fired up all at once, at the thought that a fellow like him should try and get the wind up because we were strangers to the country, but the Scotch blood and dourness were still there.

We got into another hall where we waited until time to get the boat to take us all to the various stations to get our trains. The stories of Ellis Island that are told in the Old Country so far as we could see, are all lies. I came through it with my big coat on and my bag in my hand. Nan and James had no trouble either. The doctors said James was a fine chubby little fellow.

We got on board the barge to take is to the station, arrived there, were put into a large waiting room, where we could get eatables to buy, but not allowed out until train time. Everything is for safety, for fear if you do go out, that some of the "shirks" get a hold of you.

Train time came, and we were taken to the train by the Station Master. We are shown our seats. I was going to sit in beside Nan and James, but he told me to leave that seat for the wife and baby. The carriage was a long one, with seats the same as seats on the top of cars at home, only with springs and covered with green velvet.

George Mckenzie was sitting behind Nan and I was in front. There being so many foreigners in the train George says, "We can't all sleep at once, so when you go to sleep I'll watch, and then I'll have a sleep and you watch." We found George Mckenzie to be a very true, good friend to us. He had sandwiches in his bag, and he kept us going with these until they were finished and carried drinks to us all night. The water was ice cold, and it was very enjoyable. There were paper tumblers which we had to drink out of, and they were alright.

***

We left New York at 7 p.m. on Saturday and arrived at Pittsburg at 12.30 mid day Sunday. The greatest sight we saw was the horse shoe bend on the railroad. It was a great sight. We were coming over the mountains when we saw it.

There are four railroad tracks, two for passenger trains and two for Mineral trains. The engines are much bigger and more powerful than at home. Carriages are on a larger scale also. When we came to the horse shoe bend we got another engine to give us a pull up the Hill. I can tell you they travel to some tune, but when they are stopping or starting, they do so with a jerk.

When we got to Pittsburg, the Station Master was waiting on us. I came up the platform with him and he asked me what boat I came in. I told him the "California."

"I saw it landing," he said. "I was at New York for my holidays for a fortnight."

He talked very nice and wanted James to shake hands, but James wouldn't do it. Then he took us up a side walk in the station, until he found out where we were all going. He told us when we would get our train, and told us also to be there half an hour before train time so that he would get us fixed up alright.

Just as I was about to go and see about a place to get a wash up and some dinner, another porter standing by said, "Where are you going again?" I said "Charleroi."

"Then you get a train at 1.50 p.m. or if you want to go and have a wash up you can get a train at 4 p.m."

I said I would just go and get the first train, and get to my journey's end. We took good byes with some friends we met on the boat, and left to get our train.

On the train they took our tickets, and gave us another one, which they stick in your hat, and you have no trouble: when they come to the station or just about it, they take the ticket and tell you that you go out at the next station. I thought it strange to have a ticket put in my hat, but it is where they all carry them here.

***

When we arrived at Charleroi it was 2.30 p.m. Sunday afternoon. We were met by Sammy Anderson and Joe Kerr, who gave is a heart hand shake, and then five minutes later we arrived at the house.

The table was sitting spread with all the various dainties, etc. We had a wash up first and then did justice to the eatables which disappeared from before me at the double.

I was ready for a tuck in, and I tucked in all I could, of course all the while

answering questions about friends in the Old Country, all about old times, etc.

We sat talking for hours but before it got too late, Sammy says to me at 6 o'clock "we'll go and see about a job for you." He took me to a Mr. Miller who is the Employer of labour for the Tube Mill. He shook hands and told me to come out the following day, but I told him I couldn't as the boxes hadn't arrived yet.

"Well," he says. "Whenever they come, you just come out."

I feel very thankful to God for journeying mercies, for good friends, for getting work so soon, for Health and Strength, and for everything we have received at His hands. Knowing also, that the prayers of many friends in the Old Country were going on our behalf. To them we are very grateful for their thoughtfulness.

Thus ended our journey from "Bellshill, Lanarkshire, Scotland to Cherleroi, Washington County, Pennsylvania, U.S. America.

THE CROSS, BELLSHILL

Bellshill
Lanarkshire County
Scotland

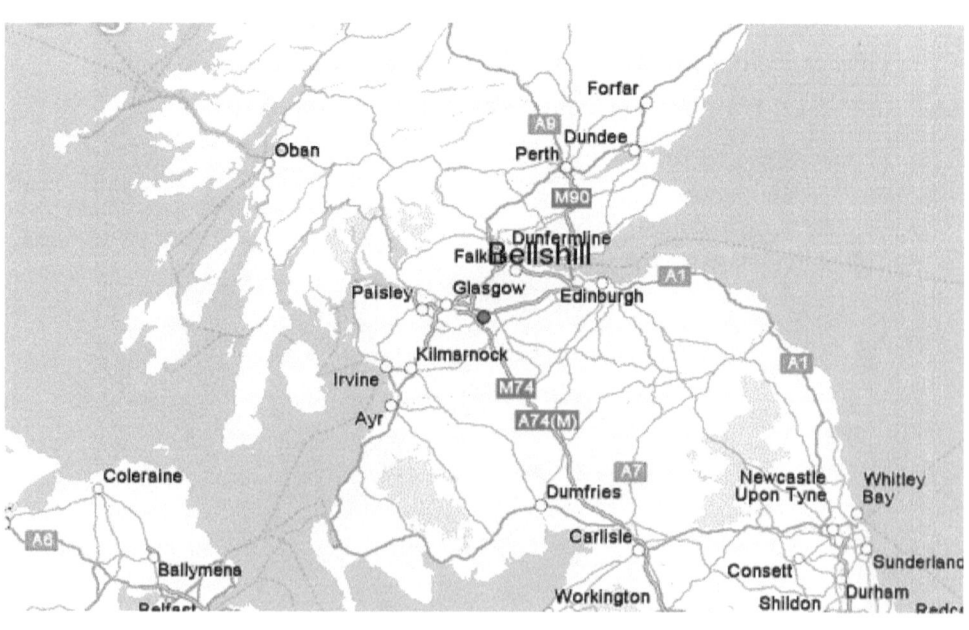

LIST OR MANIFEST OF ALIEN PASSENGERS FOR THE UNITED

ALL ALIENS arriving at a port of continental United States from a foreign port or a port of the insular possessions of the United States, and all aliens arriving at a port of said insular possessions from a foreign port

This (white) sheet is for the Notice of

S.S. "CALIFORNIA", Passengers sailing from _____ GLASGOW _____, ____ SEPTEMBER ____, 19 23.

No.	HEAD-TAX STATUS	NAME IN FULL		Age	Sex	Married or single	Calling or occupation	Able to — Read	Able to — What language	Nationality (Country of which citizen or subject)	Race or people	Last permanent residence Country	Last permanent residence City or town	The name and complete address of nearest relative or friend in country whence came	Final destination State	Final destination City or town
		Family name	Given name													
	Usher	David Gray	38	M	M	Coal Miner	Yes	English	Yes	Britain	Scotch	Scotland	Glasgow	Wife: Mrs. Mary Usher, 30, McEwan St., Parthead, Glasgow	Pa.	Pittsburgh.
2	McDonald	Mary	36	F	M	wife House-	Yes	English	Yes	Britain	Scotch	Scotland	Glasgow	Father: Robert Heart,	Pa.	Scranton.
3 UNDER 16	McDonald	Mary	4	F	S	Nil	No	Nil	No	Britain	Scotch	Scotland	Glasgow	25, Holland St.,	Pa.	Scranton.
4 UNDER 16	McDonald	Jessie	2	F	S	Nil	No	Nil	No	Britain	Scotch	Scotland	Glasgow	Glasgow.	Pa.	Scranton.
5 UNDER 16	McDonald	Sarah	2	F	S	Nil	No	Nil	No	Britain	Scotch	Scotland	Glasgow		Pa.	Scranton.
6	Corrigan	Patrick	26	M	M	Laborer	Yes	English	Yes	Britain	Scotch	Scotland	Glasgow	Wife: Mrs. Jane Corrigan, 464, Dumbarton Rd.,	Pa.	Beaver Falls
7	Corrigan	James	16	M	S	Nil	Yes	English	Yes	Britain	Scotch	Scotland	Glasgow	Belcair,	Pa.	Beaver Falls
8	Casey	John James	24	M	S	Plumber	Yes	English	Yes	Britain	Scotch	Scotland	Glasgow	Father: Daniel Casey, 127 Thistle Street, Glasgow.	Ida.	Boise
9	Christie	George	20	M	S	Laborer	Yes	English	Yes	Britain	Scotch	Scotland	Glasgow.	Father: George Christie, 127 Thistle Street, Glasgow	Mass.	Lowell.
10	Connor	William George	23	M	S	Boiler maker	Yes	English	Yes	Britain	Scotch	Scotland	Glasgow	Mother: Mrs. Frances Connor, 446, Argyle St., Glasgow.	N.Y.	New York.
11	Connor	John	20	M	M	Joiner	Yes	English	Yes	Britain	Scotch	Scotland	Glasgow	Wife: Mrs. Frances Connor, 446, Argyle St., Glasgow.	N.Y.	New York.
12	McGuire	William	21	M	M	Miner	Yes	English	Yes	Britain	Scotch	Scotland	Glentyre	Wife: Mrs. Margaret McGuire, 506, Glasgow Rd., Glentyre.	Ohio.	Columbus.
13	Addie	Andrew	31	M	M	Miner House-	Yes	English	Yes	Britain	Scotch	Scotland	Bellshill	Mother: Mrs. Mary Addie,	Pa.	Charleroi.
14	Addie	Nan	32	F	M	wife	Yes	English	Yes	Britain	Scotch	Scotland	Bellshill	111, Bothwell Park,	Pa.	Charleroi.
15	Addie	James	48	M	S	Nil	No	Nil	No	Britain	Scotch	Scotland	Bellshill	Bellshill,	Pa.	Charleroi.
16	Alcroft	Albert Edward	31	M	M	Riveter	Yes	English	Yes	Britain	Scotch	Scotland	Prestwick	Wife: Mrs. Helen Alcroft, 19, Pleasantfield Sq., Prestwick	N.Y.	Schenectady
17	Allan	William Farquhar	27	M	S	Electrical Engineer	Yes	English	Yes	Britain	Scotch	Scotland	Stonehaven	Mother: Mrs. Marion Allan, 25, Mair Terr., Stonehaven	Wisc.	Milwaukee.
18	Allison	Duncan	25	M	S	Cabinet maker	Yes	English	Yes	Britain	Scotch	Scotland	Paisley	Father: John Allison, 5, Forbes Pl., Paisley.	N.J.	Kearney.
19	Anderson	Archibald	23	M	S	Machinist	Yes	English	Yes	Britain	Scotch	Scotland	Bordeaux	Wife: Mrs. Bridget Anderson, Lamont Rd., Bridge of	N.J.	Bordertown
20	Anderson	Frances Catto	26	M	M	man	Yes	English	Yes	Britain	Scotch	Scotland	Derry	Wife: Mrs. Frances Esther Anderson c/o Brown, Woodburn, Selkirk.	N.J.	Paterson.
21	Anderson	Helen Young	26	F	M	Draughts-	Yes	English	Yes	Britain	Scotch	Scotland	Clydebank	Mother: Mrs. Margaret Young, 27, Aberconway St., Clydebank.	N.Y.	Schenectady
22	Anderson	James	27	M	M	man	Yes	English	Yes	Britain	Scotch	Scotland	Saltcoats.	Father: James Anderson, 50, Mellpark Rd., Saltcoats.	N.Y.	New York.
23	Anderson	John	22	M	S	Grocer	Yes	English	Yes	Britain	Scotch	Scotland	Paisley	Father: David Anderson, 8, Backhill Rd., Paisley.	R.I.	Pawtucket.
24	Baird	Alexander	19	M	S	Butcher	Yes	English	Yes	Britain	Scotch	Scotland	Paterhead	Father: George Baird, 29, North St., Paterhead.	N.J.	Clifton
25	Anderson	Harry Beveridge	27	M	S	man	Yes	English	Yes	Britain	Scotch	Scotland	Glasgow	Father: James Anderson, 143, Seord St., Glasgow.	N.Y.	Woodhaven, L.I
26	Barbour	John Donald	21	M	S	Draughts- Black- smith	Yes	English	Yes	Britain	Scotch	Scotland	Paisley	Wife: Mrs. Agnes Barbour, 7, Hawkhead St., Paisley	N.J.	Ridgefield
27	Baron	Polly	51	F	S	Tailoress	Yes	English	Yes	Britain	Jewish	Scotland	Glasgow	Father: Abraham Baron, 250, Main St., Glasgow, sec.	N.Y.	New York.
28	Bennie	Robert Smith	19	M	S	Clerk	Yes	English	Yes	Britain	Scotch	Scotland	Coatpoints	Mother: Mrs. Isabella Bennie, 34, Canal St., Coatpoints	R.I.	Kearney.
29	Bicker	Diana	22	F	M	wife House-	Yes	English	Yes	Britain	Scotch	Scotland	Clydebank	Mother: Mrs. Jane Tainsch, 11, Newhall St., Brigeton, Glasgow.	Mass.	New Bedford
30 UNDER 16	Bicker	James	4	M	S	Nil	No	Nil	No	Britain	Scotch	Scotland	Clydebank		Mass.	New Bedford

81

5

Total passengers . . . . . .
U.S. citizens . . . . . .

SS California Manifest of Passengers to the United States, September 26, 1923

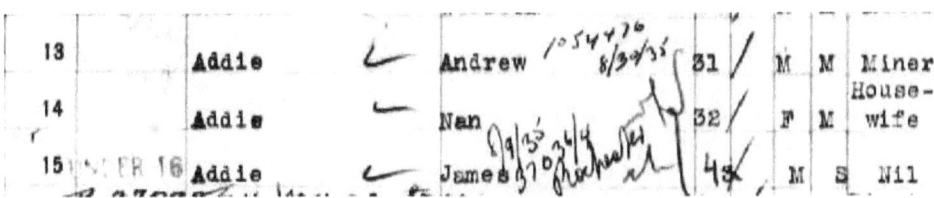

13	Addie	Andrew	31	M	M	Miner
14	Addie	Nan	32	F	M	House-wife
15	Addie	James	48	M	S	Nil

Magnification of Addie Family on Ship Manifest

City of Charleroi
Washington County
Pennsylvania

Pennsylvania

GLOSSARY

American Dry Hash: American hash browns. This specialty was also
served on the

RMS Titanic.

Bis-nap: A frozen dessert named after the town of Bisnap,
Denmark.

Dole Fish: A cousin to the dolphin. Due to its large lung size
these fish cannot

underwater and need to remain on the surface.

Dulcimer: An hourglass shaped, plucked-stringed musical
instrument with 3 - 8 strings.

Sago: Tapioca-type pudding.

Tinnie: Small tin cup or bowl.